WALES
TRAVEL
2024

EXPLORING THE LAND OF LEGENDS

CONTENTS

01 WELCOME
04 FACTS
14 DESTINATIONS
63 FOODS
87 CULTURES
91 TRAVEL ADVICES

WELCOME TO WALES

Nestled on the western edge of the British Isles, Wales welcomes you with open arms to a land steeped in history, brimming with natural wonders, and enriched by its vibrant culture. As you embark on this journey through the heart of Wales, let us extend a warm and heartfelt "Croeso i Gymru" – Welcome to Wales!

Wales, often referred to as Cymru in its native tongue, is a place of enchantment where ancient castles, rolling hills, and dramatic coastlines come together to create a tapestry of breathtaking landscapes. It's a land where the tales of knights and dragons merge with modern-day adventures and artistic expressions.

But Wales is more than just a place on the map; it's a nation with a soul. It's a place where the echoes of the past resonate in every stone, where the melodies of a resilient culture continue to thrive, and where the warmth of its people can brighten even the rainiest day.

In the pages that follow, we invite you to explore the very essence of Wales. We'll take you on a journey through its diverse regions, each with its own unique charm and character. From the bustling streets of Cardiff to the serene shores of Anglesey, from the towering peaks of Snowdonia to the hidden valleys of the Brecon Beacons, Wales offers a world of wonders waiting to be uncovered.

Whether you're an intrepid explorer seeking outdoor adventures, a history buff eager to unravel the stories of centuries gone by, or simply a traveler in search of new horizons, Wales has something extraordinary to offer you.

Prepare to be captivated by tales of legendary heroes, enchanted by the melodies of harps and choirs, and enthralled by landscapes that seem almost otherworldly. We've crafted this travel guide to be your faithful companion on this Welsh odyssey, providing you with insights, recommendations, and practical advice to make your journey through Wales an unforgettable experience.

So, as you turn the page and venture further into this guide, you'll embark on a voyage of discovery through the wonders of Wales. From its welcoming capital city to its hidden treasures, you'll soon understand why Wales is a land that captures the hearts of all who visit.

Croeso i Gymru – Welcome to Wales, where the adventure begins, and memories are made!!!

WALES

FACTS

The basics:

- Population: 3.1 million people. 4.6 per cent of the UK population.
- Location: Wales is on the island of Great Britain, to the west of England.
- Size: Around 8,023 square miles (20,779 km2) in area
- Time Zone: GMT
- Currency: Pound Sterling
- National Day: St David's Day, 1 March
- National symbols: The dragon, daffodil and leek are three of a number of national symbols.
- National Anthem: Hen Wlad fy Nhadau (Land of my Fathers)

- Government: Devolved Government with a First Minister, Cabinet and elected Parliament who meet in the Senedd (parliament) in Cardiff Bay.
- Language: Welsh and English – Wales is a bilingual country.
- Cities: There are currently six cities in Wales. Cardiff (Caerdydd in Welsh) the capital city of Wales has a population of around 363,000 and is located on the South East coast. To the east lies Newport (Casnewydd) and to the west is Swansea (Abertawe). Bangor – on the Menai Strait – overlooks the island of Anglesey, in North West Wales. St Davids in Pembrokeshire has a population of under 2000 and is the smallest city in the UK and on 14 March 2012, St Asaph, in North East Wales was awarded city status as part of the Queen's Diamond Jubilee celebrations.

Geography and climate:

- Highest mountain: Yr Wyddfa (Snowdon), Eryri (Snowdonia National Park), at 1,085m (3,560ft).
- Biggest natural lake: Llyn Tegid
- National Parks: Wales has three National Parks, which cover 20 per cent of the country's land mass and five Areas of Outstanding Natural Beauty.

Pembrokeshire Coast National Park
Eryri (Snowdonia) National Park
Bannau Brycheiniog (Brecon Beacons) National Park

- Longest placename: Llanfairpwllgwyngyllgogerychwyrndrobwllllantysiliogogogoch is the full name, which means The Church of St Mary in the hollow of the white hazel near the rapid whirlpool and the church of St Tysilio near a red cave, and it is often shortened to Llanfairpwll or Llanfair PG.
- Climate: Wales' weather is mild and variable - with average temperatures of around 20°C (68°F) in summer, and 6°C (43°F) at low altitude in the winter months.

Transport and travel:

- Wales is well-connected to the rest of the UK, Ireland and mainland Europe via road, rail, sea and air.
- Cardiff is around two hours from London travelling by road or train.

15 Intriguing Facts about Wales you should know

1. Wales is a country that is part of the United Kingdom

Have you ever wondered, "is Wales a country?" Fear not, you're not alone!
Wales was a principality for a brief period, which is why so many people question if Wales is a country or not. According to the Oxford Dictionary, a "principality" is a nation ruled by a prince.
In modern Wales, the country is governed by elected officials not by a hereditary royal prince. Wales, which is a part of the island of Great Britain and shares a border with England, is therefore a nation itself.

2. There are 7 cities in Wales

Our next Welsh fact relates to how many cities there are in Wales. The answer is 7!
Wales is home to 7 multi-sized cities that are dotted across the landscape, from south to north. The capital city of Cardiff is the oldest city in Wales, and the latest addition to Wales's collection of cities is Wrexham.
Wrexham became Wales's seventh city following a competition, which was part of the Queen's Platinum Jubilee celebrations. In Wrexham, you'll find the world's oldest international football stadium that still hosts international matches, The Racecourse. Continuing to impress, the club was famously acquired by Hollywood stars Ryan Reynolds and Rob McElhenney in 2021!

The remaining cities in Wales are Newport, Swansea, Bangor, St Asaph and St David's, all of which have distinctive traits and histories!

3. Wales has a population of over 3 million

Ever wondered how many people live in Wales? According to the 2021 census, the population of Wales was estimated to be 3,107,500 – the largest population ever recorded in Wales!
It states that the population has grown by 44,000 since the 2011 census and that 51.2% of the population were women, and 47.9% were men.

4. The size of Wales is 20,779 km²

With a collection of towering mountains, incredible beaches and miles of farmland and forests, our next fact about Wales may come as a surprise!
The size of Wales is just 20,779 km², which is arguably relatively small when we compare it to the size of England, at 243,6010 km².
However, 20,779 km² is the equivalent of 14 million rugby-size pitches, which is quite impressive!

5. Wales's National Day is St David's Day

St David's Day/Dydd Dewi Sant is a day of music, culture and language, celebrated annually on the 1st of March.
In honour of St David, this Welsh national celebration is one of the most colourful days on the calendar. It is custom to wear a daffodil or a leek, which are two of Wales' national emblems and children dress in traditional costume.

Fuel your day of celebration with traditional Welsh foods, including Welsh cakes and cawl! Afterwards, partake in several parades across Wales, including the National St David's Day Parade, which takes place in the centre of Cardiff.
See a sea of red dragons and the flag of St David, as the non-military parade brings together several cultural groups to join an imaginative celebration of Welsh heritage and culture.

6. The corgi dog originates from Wales

Yes, that's right, Queen Elizabeth II's beloved dogs hail from Wales!
The Pembroke Welsh corgi ancestry is said to date back to the 10th century and despite their tiny size, they have been used for herding for decades!
Interestingly, Welsh legend says that they are an "enchanted" breed and serve as the steed for fairy warriors.
Another Welsh fact, the origin of the name "corgi" is hard to determine! Some interpret the Welsh word "cor" to mean dwarf and "gi" as a form of the Welsh word dog.
Combine those meanings together and you have a dwarf dog! Others interpret the Welsh word "cor" to mean gather or watch over, hence their herding reputation!

7. The red, white and green dragon flag was officially recognised in 1959

The Welsh flag that we know and love – a striking red dragon on a green and white background – was officially recognised in 1959.

The dragon incorporates the red dragon of Cadwaladr, King of Gwynedd, along with the Tudor colours of red and green.
The dragon has been associated with Wales for centuries before Cadwaladr's reign; however, the origin of the symbol has been lost in myth.
Moreover, others suggest that the green and white colours represent the leek, the national emblem of Wales.

8. One of the best beach bars in the world can be found in Wales

This fact about Wales may come as a surprise, but Ty Coch Inn found itself on the official list of the best beach bars in the world!
Ty Coch, which can be found on the Llŷn Peninsula, started life as a vicarage in 1823 before it was opened as an inn in 1842, to feed the hungry shipbuilders who worked on the beach!
Today, however, this hidden beach will see thirsty patrons walk nearly a mile across the beach or across the golf course. After the small trek, you are rewarded with striking views of Snowdonia and Ireland. Children can enjoy the sandy beach and calm waters, while the adults linger over a pint and savour the surroundings!

9. Wales has more castles per square mile than anywhere else in Europe

Often referred to as the 'Castle Capital of the World', Wales has more castles per square mile than anywhere else in Europe.

With more than 600 castles in Wales to discover, almost every corner of the country has an impressive feat of architecture. From the star of 2020 and 2021's I'm a Celebrity...Get Me Out of Here! series, Gwyrch Castle in North Wales, to the fairytale setting of Castell Coch in South Wales.

10. World-famous author Roald Dahl was born in Cardiff

Another interesting fact about Wales is that despite being a relatively small country, it is home to a number of famous faces!
We all know that Tom Jones is a Welsh hero, but did you know that the children's novelist, Roald Dahl was Welsh too?
Roald Dahl was born in 1916 and Cardiff was the focal point of the writer's early life. His family lived in a substantial home, Villa Marie on Fairwater Road, which is today marked by a blue plaque for visitors to recognise.
Moreover, the Welsh city knows no shortage of Welsh talent, with Shirley Bassey and Charlotte Church also born in Cardiff!

11. Wales is home to one of the smallest cathedral cities in the world

No bigger than a village on the coastline of Pembrokeshire lies the tiny city of St Davids. St Davids is in fact the smallest city in the UK and is the seventh smallest in the world!

The city is built around the 6th-century cathedral and was granted city status by the HM Queen by Royal Charter on 1st June 1995.

The tiny city is surrounded by beautiful coastal scenery, renowned for its abundance of wildlife and gorgeous beaches. The area is also rich in early Christian heritage, with it being the site of St David's monastery and where St Patrick is said to have set sail to Ireland.
Another interesting fact about Wales!

12. Pistyll Rhaeadr is Britain's tallest single-drop waterfall

At 240ft, Pistyll Rhaeadr is Britain's tallest single-drop waterfall, resting in the Berwyn Mountains. Sitting just four miles away from the charming village of Llanrhaeadr-ym-Mochnant in Powys, the enchanting waterfall attracts many visitors each year.
This is a great spot for a flying visit or if you're feeling more adventurous, find a collection of walks surrounding. From the short stroll to the top of the waterfall to the challenging 7 miles Ridge walk. Afterwards, venture to the tearoom, which boasts many original 18th-century features. Here, you can cosy around the fire with a hot chocolate or admire water with an ice cream in hand.

13. Anglesey is the largest island in both England and Wales

Anglesey is by far the largest island in England and Wales and the seventh largest in the British Isles. Separated from mainland Wales by the famous Menai Strait, Anglesey covers an area of 261 square miles and includes Holy Island. Holy Island sits on Anglesey's western edge and is littered with its own collection of coves, headlands and bays.

On Anglesey, you will find an array of beaches, walks and unusual places to stay. As well as the small tidal island of Ynys Llanddwyn, where St Dwynwen is said to have lived!

14. The Welsh town of Llanfairpwllgwyngyllgogerychwyrndrobwllllantysiliogogogoch is the second-longest place name in the world!

Despite its impressive 58-letter name, this Welsh village is the second-longest name in the world! Second to a hill in the North Island of New Zealand, which has an 85-letter name!
Originally, the Isle of Anglesey village was just Llanfair Pwllgwyngyll. But in the 1860s it acquired a new name to draw in railway tourists. Even today, this 19th-century strategy is paying off with flocks of people visiting for the photo opportunity.
The 58-letter English translation of this Welsh word is 'The Church of Mary in the Hollow of the White Hazel Near the Fierce Whirlpool and the Church of Tysilio by the Red Cave'.

15. Wales is the only country with a complete coastal path

Wales is the only country in the world to have a continuous waymarked path along its entire coastline! On this coastal path, you can enjoy 870 miles of an unspoilt and unbroken path along the Welsh coastline. This path is promised to be much quieter than Cornwall and Devon's. The coastal path takes you from Chepstow in the south, all the way to the English board near Chester, in the north.

WALES
DESTINATIONS

1. Cardiff City (Cardiff) – Best cities to visit in Wales

Cardiff is the capital city of Wales and one of the best places to visit in Wales. It is a great city to visit and perfect for a city break with some added extras.

Cardiff is well known for its nightlife and things to do in Cardiff during the day include Cardiff Castle and walking around Cardiff Bay.

Cardiff is a good base to see more of South Wales from, you can do day trips from Cardiff to visit many places on this list of places to go in South Wales like the Brecon Beacons and Swansea Gower.

2. Castle Coch (Cardiff) – Best Castles in Wales

Another great stop on your way into or out of Cardiff is Castle Coch, one of the best castles in Europe, not only Wales!

Castle Coch is a really impressive castle and as you drive towards it, it looks like a fairytale castle sticking out of the woods! It's a 19th-century Gothic Revival castle built to protect Cardiff.

You can go inside the castle by purchasing a ticket however it is impressive to see from the outside and you can also go for a walk around the woods of Fforest Fawr where it's located.

It's one of the great things to do on a Wales trip with kids!

3. Tenby (Pembrokeshire) – Best seaside destination in Wales

Pembrokeshire is the top holiday destination in Wales, and Tenby is the most popular beach and seaside town in Pembrokeshire.

This extremely colourful town has everything you need for a Welsh seaside holiday includes Tenby holiday cottages, 3 sand beaches, coastal walks, shops, restaurants and boat tours.

I really recommend visiting Tenby on your Wales holiday because it is such a popular place and so many people love it as one of the best places to visit in Wales.

Another reason Tenby and the places near Tenby are so good is because you can base yourself here to see more of Pembrokeshire from in an easy way.

4. Saundersfoot (Pembrokeshire) – Best beaches in Pembrokeshire

Saundersfoot has a beautiful, big, sandy beach with a pretty seaside village and it's really close to Tenby. In fact, one of my favourite South Wales walks is walking from Saundersfoot to Tenby!

Saundersfoot is home to some amazing food and restaurants you should visit here when in Wales if you want a less touristic beach but still one with good holiday facilities around you.

5. Manorbier (Pembrokeshire) – Best beaches to visit in Wales

Manorbier Beach is one of the beaches near Tenby and the one of the best beaches in Wales. It's popular with locals and holidaymakers from nearby accommodation and holiday parks!

It's a great beach for beginner surfing, and surfing for children because of its small waves. It has a rock and sand beach and is surrounded by a beautiful coastal path.

Whilst stopping in Manorbier on your Wales trip, you can also visit Manorbier Castle and get some cake at Beach Break Tearooms!

6. Barafundle Bay (Pembrokeshire) - Best beaches in Wales

Voted one of the beaches in the world, Barafundle Bay is a must-visit for beautiful places in Wales.

The reason why this beach and bay is so nice is because you need to walk 10-15 minutes over a field and cliff top to get there and once you are there there are no beach facilities.

7. Bosherston Lilly Ponds (Pembrokeshire)

This is a lovely and surprising walking loop from the very small village of Bosherston. From the car park, you are a minute from a beautiful pond and footpath that takes between 1-2 hours to walk around.

Not many people know about the Bosherston Lilly Ponds because they are hidden, so they are definitely a hidden gem in Wales that you need to keep in mind when planning where to go in Wales!

8. St Govan's Chapel (Pembrokeshire) – Best hidden gems in Wales

If you want to visit more hidden gems in Wales, St Govan's Chapel is another place to visit!

This is a chapel hidden down a set of steps that leads out onto a hidden bay!

It's really close to Bosherston Lilly Ponds so you should plan to visit both at one time on your Wales itinerary.

9. Freshwater West Beach (Pembrokeshire)

If you're a Harry Potter fan you may know of this beach because it is where Dobby the house-elf is laid to rest after his battle!

There is a little memorial for Dobby with rocks and stones behind the dunes that you can visit which is a must-visit for Harry Potter fans in South Wales!

You should still visit this beach in Pembrokeshire even if you are not a Harry Potter fan because it is another one of Pembrokeshire's best beaches. I visited at sunset and it was such an amazing sunset spot so try to include this on your itinerary for Wales too!

10. Pembroke Castle (Pembrokeshire) – Best Castles in Wales

Pembroke town is not somewhere you need too spend much time but whilst travelling through Pembrokeshire in Wales, you may find yourself passing through Pembroke and Pembroke Castle is a nice place to stop.

There are so many castles in Wales and Pembroke Castle is one of the big castles that you can fully walk around so it's one of the great things to do in Pembrokeshire with kids.

When in Pembroke town you can also take a walk along the river and get lunch or a drink in one of the many pubs close to the castle.

11. Oakwood Theme Park (Pembrokeshire)
– Best family activities in Wales

This is Wales biggest theme park and therefore the biggest of the Wales tourist attractions. From my many experiences there as a teenager, a really good theme park too!

If you want to do something a bit different or it is not beach weather, you can have fun at Oakwood theme park!

12. Ramsey Island (Pembrokeshire) – Best islands to visit in Wales

Ramsey Island is one of the beauty spots in Wales. You can see and visit Ramsey Island on a boat trip. I booked this whilst in St David's which is the small city nearby.

In the right season you can spot whales and dolphins from the boat and I believe all year round you'll get to see seals which is what I saw. It's a great day out in South Wales and Pembrokeshire for children and adults!

13. Blue Lagoon (Pembrokeshire) – Best places to swim in Wales

If you want somewhere cool to swim in Wales, especially in the summer, you have to add the Blue Lagoon to your list of top places to visit in South Wales!

It's a former slate quarry and now features a big, and deep, lagoon that is popular for coasteering, kayaking and swimming!

To find it, you need to search and head to: National Trust – Abereiddi to Abermaw. You won't find 'Blue Lagoon Wales' as a point on Google Maps.

The Blue Lagoon is now one of the South Wales Instagram spots you see a lot of online!

14. Pen Y Fan (Brecon Beacons National Park) – Best hikes in Brecon Beacons

The Brecon Beacons National Park is definitely one of the top places to visit in Wales because of its stunning countryside, its activities and hikes!

The Brecon Beacons is the best place for hiking in South Wales, it has the second-highest peak in Wales called Pen Y Fan (the highest peak is Snowdon in North Wales).

Hiking Pen Y Fan makes for a brilliant day out in Wales and I really recommend taking on the challenge to tick this well known peak off and see South Wales from above!

15. Hay on Wye (Brecon Beacons National Park)
– Prettiest towns in Wales

You'll find the pretty market town of Hay on Wye in the Brecon Beacons National Park to the North on the edge of England and Wales.

Hay on Wye is a really unique place making it one of the places of interest in Wales because it is famous for its literature and books!

The town is full of book shops old and new along with other independent shops and lots of nice cafes. It's a real gem in South Wales!

16. Brecon Beacons Waterfalls (Brecon Beacons National Park) – Best Waterfalls in Wales

When looking for famous Welsh places to visit, how can you leave Brecon Beaons National Park. It is full of waterfalls and if you're looking for where to visit in Wales, I recommend going to see some waterfalls in the National Park.

There is a 4 waterfall walk which is a popular walk and relatively easy walk to do taking just a few hours.

There are places to go wild swimming in the Brecon Beacons on the walk as well as walking behind a waterfall and seeing more of the beautiful landscape of the National Park in Wales.

17. Barry Island (Glamorgan) – Best beaches to visit in Wales for families

If you know of Gavin and Stacey, you'll know Barry Island, and for some seaside fun and for one of the popular days out in Wales you can head to Barry Island for the day!

Barry Island is full of candy floss, fish & chips, arcade games, and rides, some people think it's a bit tacky but if you go for the fun of it, you'll have a good time!

Plus, there are a few different beaches in Barry Island and some are much quieter and relaxed than others so it's still worth checking out, even if you are dubious!

18. Nash Point (Glamorgan) – Best walks in Wales

A hugely underrated part of Wales is the Glamorgan Heritage Coast! This part of the Wales Coastal Path between Cardiff and Swansea is full of amazing beaches and Wales beauty spots.

Nash Point is my favourite area on the Glamorgan Heritage Coast in South Wales.

It has a towering cliff edge and the rocks down at the beach are one of the best places in ways for fossil hunting in Wales! If you have children who are into dinosaurs, this is a great stop in Wales!

19. Merthyr Mawr Sand Dunes (Glamorgan)
– Best hidden places in Wales

For a super unique walk in Wales, check out the Merthyr Mawr Nature Reserve featuring huge sand dunes.. yes sand dunes!

My sister goes walking here with her dogs all the time and I only recently found out about it because it is a spot only locals know!

Head to Merthyr Mawr Nature Reserve on Google Maps here. As you reach this point, you'll get to the car park and from there you'll see the big sand dunes you need to climb!

You can choose the steep dunes or some easier sand dunes and once at the top you'll be rewarded with an incredible coastline view over Merthyr Mawr Beach and you can keep walking around the nature reserve from here which is easier to walk since you've already passed the sand dunes!

20. Cowbridge (Glamorgan) – Most beautiful towns in Wales

Cowbridge is a lovely market town between Cardiff and Bridgend so if you're driving from Cardiff to the Glamorgan Heritage Coast I suggest you take the scenic route rather than the M4 and drive through Cowbridge.

It's full of independent shops in colourful buildings. There's a pretty garden called the Physic Garden you can stretch your legs in and I recommend getting ice cream from Fablas Ice Cream Parlour.

It's a hidden gem in Wales for sure!

21. Rhossili Bay (Swansea Gower) – Best beaches to visit in Wales

The Swansea Gower feels like an Island off of the coast of Swansea and South Wales but it is actually joined to the mainland making it easy to visit from the M4.

Rhossili Bay is the most famous place to visit on the Gower because this beach has been voted as one of the best beaches in Wales (and maybe the world?). It's not hard to see why so it should be on your list of places to visit in Wales!

The beach is huge and you get an amazing view of it whilst taking a coastal walk down Worms Head.

22. Three Cliffs Bay (Swansea Gower) – Best beach walks in Wales

Another one of the best beaches in Swansea Gower is the Three Cliffs Bay which offers you a wild beach experience with sand dunes, a salt marsh and limestone cliffs, plus an amazing sand beach.

You can base yourself here for a few days on your Wales trip, the Three Cliffs Bay Holiday Park is a well known and popular place to stay in Wales or you can stop by whilst visiting the other places to go in South Wales on this list.

23. National Botanic Gardens of Wales (Carmarthenshire)
– Best gardens to visit in Wales

When planning your Wales trip, the National Botanic Gardens of Wales outside Carmarthen is a good place to stop all year round and definitely one of the good things to do in Wales when it rains because much of it is inside!

At this Wales tourist attraction you can visit the Great Glasshouse and Tropical House indoors and get a ticket for the British Bird of Prey Centre!

If the weather is good you can stretch your legs in the 400 acre Waun Las National Nature Reserve which is an enchanting mosaic of flower-rich meadows, evocative woodlands, waterfalls and cascades.

When stopping in Carmarthen, there are many nice villages near by like Llansteffan near by so be sure to plan in a few hours to see the near-by area!

24. Pembrey Country Park and Beach (Carmarthenshire)

If you're doing this Wales trip with kids and want to wear them out, or you want a really good walk yourself, Pembrey Country Park is where you need to visit.

With an 8 mile long beach and a huge woodland area there is plenty of space to walk! You can also do activities here like horse riding, Wales longest toboggan run, dry ski slopes, crazy golf and more!

If you are looking for caravan sites and camping in Wales sites, I really recommend Pembrey Campsite because of how many facilities are within the County Park.

25. Wye Valley (England Wales Border)
– Best places to visit in Wales near England

On the very edge of Wales is the Wye Valley so if you're driving from Southern England to Wales, you should pass through the Wye Valley on the way.

One of the main places to visit in the Wye Valley is Tintern Abbey. The historic Abbey ruins of Tintern Abbey and the village of Tintern are a good place to stretch your legs at the start or end of your Wales road trip as these are the famous landmark in Wales.

If you want a bit of a hike you can hike up to Devils Pulpit which is nearby and a great introduction to Wales hikes!

26. Cardigan

For places to visit in Wales, Cardigan has to be on the list! Despite Cardigan's small size, this ancient market town is a great place to base yourself in South West Wales because there are plenty of things to do in Cardigan and Cardigan Bay.

The Cardigan Bay coastline is by far the top attraction, it's actually where the Pembrokeshire Coastal Path starts so if you enjoy hiking, this is a great place to go.

Cardigan is surrounded by amazing beaches which are much less touristy than many of those further South in Pembrokeshire and you're bound to see more of Welsh local life in this part of Wales.

27. The Elan Valley (Powys)

The Powys region is technically in Mid-Wales but when looking at a map of Wales, it is closer to the South and easier to reach from South Wales, that's why this impressive place area is ending my list of places to visit in Wales!

Elan Valley and the Elan Valley Dams and Reservoirs are one of the top places to visit in Powys. They were built a hundred years ago to supply desperately needed clean water to Birmingham. Today, they are perfect for walking around and they are impressive to see with gushing water travelling from one dam to another!

If you are coming from the Midlands into South Wales, going via the Elan Valley is a good way to enter or exit Wales and see this stunning beauty spot in Wales!

28. Yr Wyddfa (Mount Snowdon) (Snowdonia National Park) – Best hikes in Wales

If the weather is on your side, climbing Yr Wyddfa (Mount Snowdon) should be on top of the list on your Wales itinerary! Yr Wyddfa (Mount Snowdon) is the highest peak in Wales and although climbing it is hard work, it is do-able for many people and such a great achievement!

There are a few routes to the top, I have done it from Pen Y Pass a few times which I recommend, and if you don't fancy the walk you can use the Snowdon Mountain Railway train to help you which is especially good if you're in North Wales with children.

29. Llanberis Eryri National Park (Snowdonia National Park) – Best places for families to visit in Wales

Llanberis is the town most people will pass through on the way to Yr Wyddfa (Mount Snowdon) and many people park in Llanberis and start the hike up Yr Wyddfa (Mount Snowdon) from here too.

Therefore if you are looking for things to do near Yr Wyddfa (Mount Snowdon), Llanberis is a good place to visit.

Llanberis has a huge lake which is popular for watersports and many families come to relax on the grassy bank along the lake which has play areas too.

Tourist attractions in Llanberis include the Llanberis Lake Railway, National Slate Museum and Dolbadarn Castle. Overall it's a perfect place for families to visit in Wales.

30. Dinorwig Quarry (Snowdonia National Park)

Also in Llanberis is Dinorwig Quarry but I'm adding this as it's own place to visit in Wales because it's a full day out on it's own.

We had a great afternoon hiking here last year. We parked up in Llanberis main car park and headed straight into the forest between the two lakes here. If you search for Dinorwig Quarry on Google maps, you'll find it easily.

We were so surprised by what we saw here. There are lots of old mining buildings within the forest, also known as the Anglesey Barracks as workers from Angelesey used to stay here. Dali's Hole is a lake right at the top of the mountain and forest which you can walk to and then you can head over into the footpaths through the old Quarry.

On google it's hard to see where to go, but trust me when you are there there are many places for walking here, with amazing views of the Yr Wyddfa (Mount Snowdon) in front.

31. Watkins Path Waterfalls (Snowdonia National Park) – Best waterfalls in Wales

Now wild swimming is all the range, one of the super unique and cool places for wild swimming in Wales and in Snowdonia is the Watkin Path Waterfalls!

The Watkins Path is another route to the top of Mount Snowdon but close-ish to the start of the walk you'll find lots of pools one after each other than run down the mountain. They're basically natural infinity pools in North Wales and the best places for swimming in Snowdonia.

32. Cwmorthin Lake, (Eryri National Park – Snowdonia National Park) – Best lakes in Wales

Eryri National Park (Snowdonia National Park) is made up of so many lakes and it will be hard to drive past them on your North Wales trip without wanting to stop! One of the good lakes to stop at is Cwmorthin Lake because of its history.

This used to be a slate mine so when you visit the lake you can see the former Cwmorthin Slate Mine, there is also Cwmorthin Waterfall down the river from the lake so it makes a great place to stop for a walk in nature.

If you fancy some wild swimming in North Wales, this place is for you too!

33. Zip-Line (Eryri National Park – Snowdonia National Park) – Best activities in Wales

One of the top places to visit in Wales for a lot of fun is Zip World in North Wales.

Zip World have 4 locations in North Wales 3 of which are in Eryri National Park (Snowdonia National Park).

The activities in each of them change from a roller coaster through the forest, sky rides, velocity ziplines and so much more, so pick which ones sound most appealing to you and book in because this will give your Wales road trip a huge adrenaline hit!

Zip World have revamped their North Wales activities quite a lot recently and now, in their Slate Cavern location in Eryri National Park (Snowdonia National Park) you can play underground golf and go on trampolines inside the cavern!

It's best to book all Zip-World activities in Wales online in advance so you don't miss out, especially for weekends and school holidays!

34. Adventure Parc Snowdonia (Snowdonia National Park) – Best attractions in Wales

Adventure Parc Snowdonia has something for everyone in the family and you don't have to have children to enjoy it! It's an adults adventure playground too!

For high class, adrenaline activities in Wales like surfing on a man-made surfing pool, rock climbing walls, high ropes, indoor caves, soft play, paddle boarding, zip lines, biking and coasteering, check Adventure Parc Snowdonia out for all of the best water activities in North Wales!

35. Mount Tryfan (Snowdonia National Park)
- Best hike in Snowdon National Park

If you are up for an intense hike, be sure to add Mount Tryfan to your list of places to go in Wales and places for hiking in North Wales.

In fact, it's not a hike, it's a scramble to the top! It took me 5 hours and although it was hard and scary at times, it was so rewarding!

36. Conway City (Conwy) – Best cities in Wales to visit

Conway is a walled market town and worth visiting a few reasons. The main reason being Conwy Castle. There are many Castles in North Wales but this one is hugely impressive and if you only visit one castle in Wales it should be this one!

Conway is also home to the smallest house in Great Britain and still has it's town walls intact so it's a great place to visit for history in Wales if you don't fancy a beach day or the weather is not on your side for exploring the wild outdoors.

37. LLandudno (Conwy) – Best seaside resorts in Wales

Llandudno is an old British seaside resort but it is still thriving today and is clean and tidy to visit.

I love the old victorian buildings that line the huge promenade and beach. Llandudno pier is easily the top of the list of Llandudno tourist attractions is a good place for some typical seaside fun!

It is a resort town so there are lots of activities near Llandudno like a ski slope and one of the popular things to do in Llandudno is to drive up to and around the Great Orme rock that stands out beside the town. Be sure to look for seals in the ocean below too!

For one of the great places to visit near Llandudno you can go to Conwy city or one of the many nearby beaches like Colwyn Bay Beach.

We have some paddle boards and recently took them out onto the sea from Llandudno beach. We found it easy to park right by the beach and get to the water carrying the boards. The water was a bit choppy for us but if it was a nice still day, this is a great paddle boarding spot in North Wales.

38. Gwrych Castle (Conwy) – Best castles in Wales to visit

Another one of the top Castles to visit in Wales is Gwrych Castle. This is one of the beautiful places in Wales to visit anyway, however it has now become even more popular due to it being where "I'm A Celebrity... Get Me Out of Here!" was filmed for two consecutive years.

You need to purchase tickets to enter Gwrych Castle and if you want to know what it's like to stay overnight in a castle, you can book to stay in one of their lodges!

39. Portmeirion Tourist Village (Gwynedd) – Best places for families to visit in Wales

Aside from Snowdon, I'd say this is the top of the list in tourist attractions in Wales.

For a slice of Italy in Wales, you can visit Portmeirion. It is a pretty iconic place so you may have seen photos of it before online and it's definitely one of the most iconic places to visit in North Wales.

It is a tourist village and it does get very busy so don't go expecting a quaint village, it also costs £12.00 per adult to enter but for a unique experience to see some nice buildings and gardens it's worth going.

Porthmadog is the closest town to Portmeirion which is quite a popular tourist town, so this place works as one of the great places to visit near Porthmadog.

40. Harlech Beach (Gwynedd) – Best beaches in Wales to visit

For one of the best beaches in Wales with a beautiful stretch of white sand and clear blue water head to Harlech Beach! It's one of the most beautiful beaches in Wales I have seen and I love that it has the sand dunes behind it.

Whilst you're in Harlech you can check out the local town and definitely take a visit to Harlech Castle which stands prominently on the hill and another great North Wales attractions.

Harlech is a good place to visit before or after Portmeirion as they are quite close together.

41. Black Rock Sands Beach (Gwynedd)
– Biggest beaches in Wales

Black Rock Sands Beach is a really cool and different beach to visit because you can drive onto it!! It's so amazing and fun, especially if you have always wanted to experience driving on a huge beach!

It costs £5.00 to enter the beach and after that, you have the whole beach to decide where to drive and park up. There is a chance you could get stuck in wet sand but there are people there to help pull you out!

This is another one of the good places to visit near Porthmadog as it isn't far away at all.

42. Aber Falls (Gwynedd) – Best waterfalls in Wales

Wales is all about waterfalls and one of the most visited waterfalls in Wales is Aber Falls! It's a great place to stop as you are leaving Snowdon to go into North England or Conwy or Llandudno because it's just off the main North Wales Expressway.

Aber Falls is popular because it is fairly easily accessible so it's good for kids to walk with an impressive waterfall at the end so get this on your list of things to see in Wales!

43. Abersoch Beach (Llyn Peninsula) – Best beaches for families in Wales

The beaches in North Wales are some of the top places to visit in North Wales all year round.

For a calm and sandy beach, Abersoch is the beach for you. You can head here in all seasons for a sunny day on the beach and a winters walk.

If you have children this is a good beach to add to your places to visit in Wales with kids as it is family friendly and safe.

44. Ty Coch Inn (Llyn Peninsula) – Best pubs in Wales

A Beach Bar might not be what you expect to see in Wales, but this is why this part of the UK is so great because it offers surprise after surprise.

Ty Coch Inn has been voted in the top ten beach bars in the world because this typical Welsh pub is located on a beautiful stretch of beach.

It's definitely one of the unique places to visit in Wales because there are not many other places you find a pub in such an incredible location.

45. Pen-Llyn Riding Centre (Llyn Peninsula)
– Best activities in Wales

If you want to add some horse riding in Wales to your list of things to do in Wales, I went out on a hack with Pen-Llyn Riding Centre last year and it was such a great way to see see this part of the Llyn Peninsula which is called Pwllheli.

46. Beaumaris (Anglesey Island) – Best islands in Wales to visit

Anglesey is an island off of the North-West coast of Wales connected by a bridge in Bangor, and if there is one place you should visit in Anglesey it's Beaumaris.

Beaumaris is a charming seaside town with a mix of medieval, Georgian, Victorian and Edwardian architecture and lots of them are painted in bright colours!

For tourist attractions in Anglesey, you can visit Beaumaris Castle, take a Puffin Island boat trip, walk along the seafront and get some fish and chips from one of the many shops!

47. Newborough Beach (Anglesey Island)
– Best sandy beaches in Wales

This is one of my favourite beaches in Wales! To get there you drive through Newborough National Nature Reserve, followed by a quick walk over sand dunes before getting to a long stretch of white sand!

The Eryri National Park (Snowdonia National Park) Mountains provide a stunning backdrop to this beach. It's perfect for water sports like kayaking and paddle boarding and you can do a great walk to the end of the peninsula to see the lighthouses.

48. South Stack Lighthouse (Anglesey Island)
– Best lighthouses in Wales

This is one of my husbands top places to visit in Wales. He just loves seeing South Stack Lighthouse perched right on the last edge of the West Coast of Wales so remotely and it's amazing that it was built in 1809.

We also love the drive to South Stack Lighthouse, it's so scenic and totally worth the extra time it takes you get here as it's a one of the best places to see in Anglesey. Once here, you can visit inside the lighthouse with a ticket, there are walking paths along the coast and you can check out Elin's Tower.

Which are the best road trips and drives in Wales?

You can't go far in Wales without experiencing great views, but if you're set on seeking out some of the very finest scenery, try these drives.

- Wye Valley: Savour the wooded gorge of the River Wye on a journey from Monmouth past Tintern Abbey to Chepstow.

- Gospel Pass: Take the narrow road over the roof of the Black Mountains from Abergavenny past Llanthony Priory to Hay-on-Wye.

- Elan Valley and Cwmystwyth: From Rhayader take the mountain road up past the reservoirs of the Elan Valley up to the blasted landscapes around Cwmystwyth and down past Devil's Bridge into the Vale of Rheidol.

- Abergwesyn Pass: Follow the ancient drovers' road over the spectacularly remote moorland of the Cambrian Mountains from Llanwrtyd Wells to Tregaron.

- Marine Drive: A short but wonderfully scenic loop around the Great Orme.

How many steam trains operate in Wales?

Currently twelve steam trains also known as heritage trains, operate in Wales together as the The Great Little Trains of Wales.

Historically with the rising demand for quarried stone in the nineteenth century, quarry and mine owners had to find more economical ways than packhorses to get their products to market, but in the steep, tortuous valleys of Snowdonia, standard-gauge train tracks proved too unwieldy.

The solution was rails, usually about 2ft apart, plied by steam engines and dinky rolling stock. The charm of these railways was recognized by train enthusiasts, and long after the decline of the quarries, they banded together to restore abandoned lines and locos. Most lines are still largely run by volunteers, who have also started up new services along unused sections of standard-gauge bed.

Tickets are generally sold separately, but The Great Little Trains of Wales offers a Discount Card giving you 20 percent off the cost of the journey on all of the Great Little trains of Wales steam train railways.

Here is our pick of the best steam trains in Wales to include in your travel, listed north to south:

1. **Snowdon Mountain Railway** Llanberis.
2. **Welsh Highland Railway** Porthmadog.
3. **Ffestiniog Railway** Porthmadog.
4. **Llangollen Railway** Llangollen.
5. **Talyllyn Railway** Tywyn.
6. **Vale of Rheidol Railway** Aberystwyth.

WALES

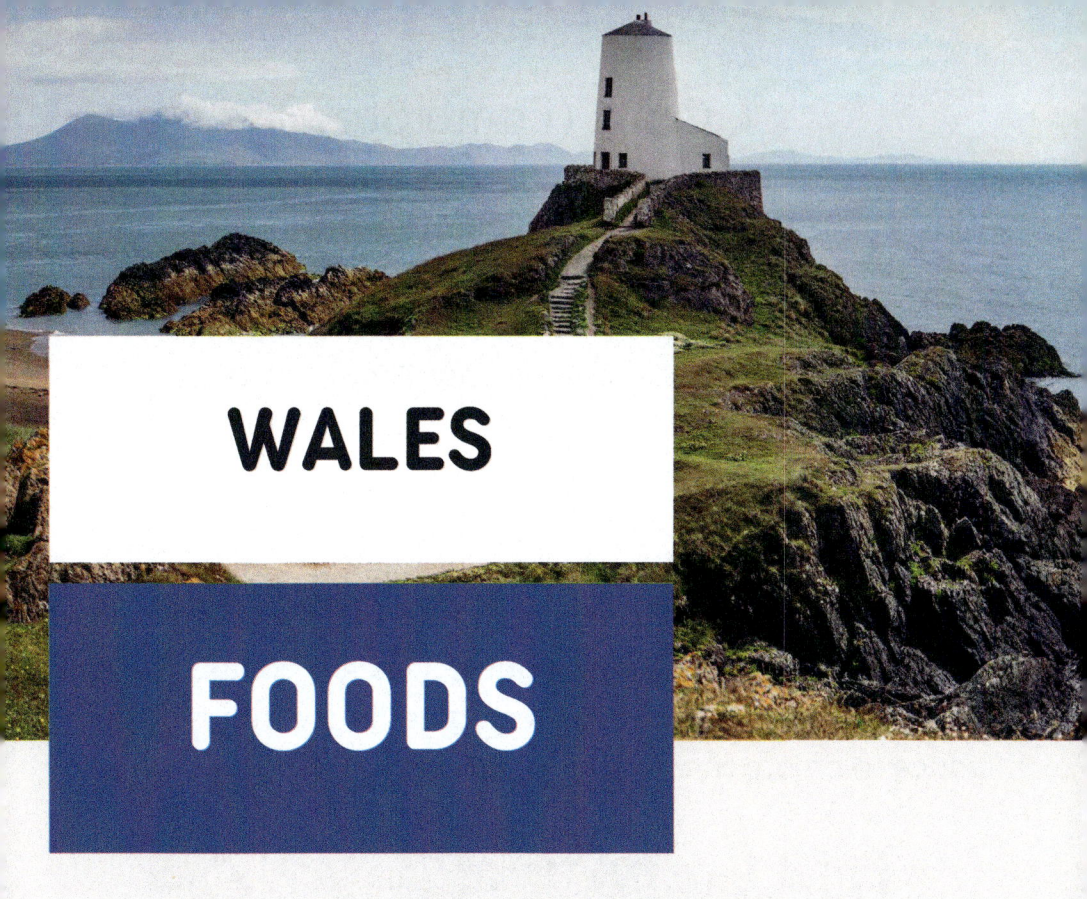

FOODS

Wales still has thousands of cafés, restaurants and pubs where you get chips with everything and a salad means a bit of wilted lettuce and a few segments of fridge-cold tomato, but it is increasingly rare to find a town where you can't find good food. Native Welsh cuisine is frequently rooted in economical ingredients, but an increasing number of menus make superb use of traditional fare, such as salt-marsh lamb, wonderful Welsh black beef, fresh salmon and sewin, frequently combined with the national vegetable, the leek. Specialities include laver bread, edible seaweed often mixed with oats then fried with a traditional breakfast of pork sausages, egg and bacon. Other dishes well worth investigating include Glamorgan sausages, cawl, and cockles, trawled from the estuary north of the Gower.

1. Cawl (Lamb Stew)

This comforting classic is a favorite among locals during the cooler months. Delicious Lamb Cawl is considered the national dish of Wales and with one bite you will understand why. This luscious and filling stew is so generous and warm that it feels like a hug for your stomach.

Lamb Cawl is a stew made from traditionally underused portions of the animal. Today many variations exist but a typical lamb cawl may use a lamb's neck or joints. The rich meat is stewed with hearty vegetables in a lightly seasoned sauce to create the perfect Welsh food!

Try this hearty stew on a cool Welsh night for a bite of true comfort.

2. Laverbread (Seaweed Spread)

Despite its name, laverbread is not actually bread. This Welsh food is a spread made from boiled seaweed. It is crafted with the lush local variety of seaweed, Laver. This is a highly prized type of seaweed known for its briny flavor and crisp texture.

The seaweed is boiled into a paste that goes wonderfully with fresh seafood or served on toast. This classic Welsh food is often spread on crusty bread and served alongside mussels.

3. Aberffraw Biscuit

This traditional Welsh food may be one of the oldest in all of the United Kingdom. The Aberffraw biscuit is a classic Welsh shortbread cookie. This sweet bite of Welsh cuisine has a texture that will make your mouth water. They are wonderfully short and crumbly thanks to plenty of creamy local dairy in their batter.

This traditional biscuit is shaped into a lovely seashell possibly as a nod to their light and sandy texture. Enjoy these beautiful biscuits with hot black tea.

4. Leek Soup

The leek is Wales' favorite vegetable. Welsh soldiers were once ordered to wear leeks on their armor as insignia and the leek has stuck as the endearing symbol of Wales. One of the best foods in Wales to celebrate the leek is deliciously creamy leek soup.

Leek soup is a delectably smooth dish typically made from leeks and potatoes. Often Welsh chefs work delicious local cheese into the soup for added creaminess. Try this creamy soup in Wales with a rarebit or toast.

5. Salt Marsh Lamb

The lush landscape of Wales supports some of the best culinary herds of lamb in the world. One particular variety of this local meat is the salt marsh lamb. This meat is seasonal and can typically be found from summer through fall only. The herds graze freely in the salt marshes making the meat rich and evenly fatted. This particular cut of lamb is known for its rich Welsh flavor.

6. Welsh Rarebit (Cheese Toast)

This Welsh food is highly loved and has been reinvented in countless ways throughout the years. Welsh rarebit is a delectable celebration of the Welsh love of cheese. It is a simple dish made from toasted bread topped with a creamy cheese sauce.

Some variations include a creamy bechamel-style sauce, whereas others have a more simple toasted cheese topper. No matter how you try it, this simple Welsh side dish will win you over.

7. Welsh Cakes

No tea is complete without delightful treats. Welsh cakes are the perfect sweet bite of food in Wales to set you up on a sweet note. These treats are sweet cakes that have been capturing Welsh hearts for centuries.

The recipe uses basic sweet cake ingredients with the addition of sweet dried fruit. The sugary cakes are made thin and pan-fried so they have nice crispy edges. Welsh cakes are perfect with warm tea or as an afternoon pick-me-up.

8. Teisennau Tatws (Potato Pancakes)

Wales is an island with a cool climate so getting crops to grow here can be challenging, but one vegetable that thrives here is the potato. These tasty spuds make the base of the delicious Welsh food of Teisennau Tatws or potato pancakes.

This savory treat is made by boiling potatoes and then mashing them with flour and spices to make dough. The dough is pressed into thin discs and then pan-fried. The delicious potato cakes get crisp and caramelized from the frying making them simply irresistible.

The welsh delicacy is excellent with breakfast or served with local lamb for dinner.

9. Crempog (Welsh Pancakes)

Crempog is an amazing Welsh dish of pancakes. These airy cakes are known throughout Wales for their satisfying chew and light sweetness.

The batter for crempog is a lot like other pancake batters, except for the addition of vinegar. This gives the batter a little acid that makes the cakes interesting and delightful. Crempog is often enjoyed with berries, syrup, honey, or whipped cream.

10. Bara Brith (Welsh Tea Bread)

This sweet Welsh food has been completing tea time in Wales for centuries. It is a beautiful traditional bread that has the perfect balance of sweetness and chew.

This traditional Welsh food utilizes the flavors of molasses and tea to craft a bread that is warmly spiced and fragrant. The bread is studded with wonderful dried fruits like currants and raisins and then baked into a beautiful brown loaf.

This bread is a classic icon of Welsh cuisine and it goes beautifully with black tea.

11. Tatws Popty (Welsh Potatoes)

This traditional Welsh food is comfort in a bowl. Tatws popty is a baked potato dish that has been enticing Welsh appetites for centuries. The original version of this dish called for the cooking of potatoes and meat together but many of today's Welsh chefs leave the meat out.

The whole dish is oven roasted to bring out the flavors of the vegetables and potatoes. This bountiful Welsh food can be served aside a lamb steak or as a meal on its own.

12. Teisen Nionod (Onion Cake)

The traditional dish of teisen nionod is packed with all the rich savory flavors you can expect from Welsh cuisine. This delicacy is an onion cake made from layers of thinly sliced potatoes and flavorful onions.

Spices and caerphilly cheese are added to the layers and the whole dish is baked into a sweet and savory onion cake. This dish in Wales is so savory and desirable you will want it alongside every dish you order here!

13. Caws (Welsh Cheese)

Arguably the most important ingredient in Welsh cuisine is the local caws or cheese. Welsh cheese is a point of pride among residents and their cheeses have some of the boldest and full-bodied flavors around.

There are lots of local cheeses to sample here but the two most popular are caerphilly and perl las. Caerphilly is an earthy and umami-packed hard cheese with a rind. It grates beautifully and tastes of mushrooms. Perl las is a blue cheese with a salty rind. Its tangy blue-cheese flavor opens into something truly sensational the more you sample.

14. Gwledd y Cybydd (Bacon and Potatoes)

This traditional food in Wales is nicknamed "the miser's feast," because of its thriftiness. This hearty basic dish is made from potatoes and bacon rashers. The two are boiled together into a meaty potato slush.

The bacon helps season the potatoes and boiling makes them smooth and sauce-like. This dish has been a fallback for the Welsh during lean times, and it goes to show that even in times of sparsity there is flavor to be found!

15. Oggie (Hand Pie)

Almost every culture has some variety of hand-held pies or pastries. The oggie is the super-sized Welsh version of a hand pie. This delightfully savory Welsh food hits all the notes, with a flaky crust and unctuous fillings making a great lunch, snack, or dinner.

The filling for oggies varies, but frequently includes lamb, leeks, onions, and potatoes. The seasonings are perfectly balanced and this dish in Wales is just right to grab and go! Enjoy an oggie as you wander through Cardiff.

16. Conwy Mussels

The bounty of the sea is a frequent theme in Welsh cuisine and one dish locals are particularly proud of is Conwy mussels. Just around the corner from Conwy Castle where freshwater meets the Atlantic, beautiful mussels grow.

This is one of the most beautifully flavored foods in Wales and it occurs naturally that way. The mussels are hand-raked and sold fresh to local markets and restaurants. Try these colorful mussels with laverbread.

17. Glamorgan Sausages (Vegetarian Sausages)

This sensational vegetarian treat has been a staple of Welsh cuisine for ages. Glamorgan sausages are not sausage at all, but rather a mince of cheese, leeks, and bread crumbs.

The star of this Welsh food is the local caerphilly cheese. It has a wonderfully earthy and nutty flavor that makes these cheesy delights just perfect!

18. Sewin and Samphire (Trout and Local Veggies)

Wales has great access to the sea and that has gifted Welsh cuisine with abundant ocean-inspired dishes. One locally loved dish is sewin and samphire.

Sewin is a local variety of trout and samphire is a succulent plant that grows along the rocky seashores in Wales. Samphire has an appearance similar to asparagus and a strong salty flavor. These two are commonly roasted and served together as a seafood delicacy.

19. Ffagadau (Meatballs and Potatoes)

The locals in Wales love meatballs. They are the perfect humble meal for any day of the week and this nostalgic meal holds a special place in Welsh cuisine.

The Welsh-style meatball typically includes a blend of pork, beef, lamb, and bacon along with spices. The delicious meatballs are cooked in a beautiful brown sauce and served with mashed potatoes.
Pair this tasty Welsh food with green peas for the perfect meal in Wales.

20. Wyau Ynys Mon (Egg and Leek Casserole)

This gorgeous Welsh food does not skip on the calories but it is a dish of true comfort! This classic Welsh casserole is made from wonderfully sweet and aromatic leeks, mashed potatoes, and hard-boiled eggs. It is a rich, decadent vegetarian dish that will make you say, "meat who?"

Eating & Drinking Travel Guide

1. Eating

Wales still has thousands of cafés, restaurants and pubs where you get chips with everything and a salad means a bit of wilted lettuce and a few segments of fridge-cold tomato, but it is increasingly rare to find a town where you can't find good food.

Native **Welsh cuisine** is frequently rooted in economical ingredients, but an increasing number of menus make superb use of traditional fare, such as salt-marsh lamb (best served minted or with thyme or rosemary), wonderful Welsh black beef, fresh salmon and sewin (sea trout), frequently combined with the national vegetable, the leek. Specialities include **laver bread** (bara lawr), edible seaweed often mixed with oats then fried with a traditional breakfast of pork sausages, egg and bacon. Other dishes well worth investigating include **Glamorgan sausages** (a spiced vegetarian combination of Caerphilly cheese, breadcrumbs and leeks), cawl (a chunky mutton broth), and cockles, trawled from the estuary north of the Gower.

The best-known of Wales' famed **cheeses** is Caerphilly, a soft, crumbly, white cheese that forms the basis of a true Welsh rarebit when mixed with beer and toasted on bread. Creamy goat's cheeses can be found all over the country, such as the superb Cothi Valley goat's cheese, as well as delicacies like organic Per Las blue cheese, and Collier's mature cheddar.

Other dairy products include ice cream, which, despite the climate, is exceptionally popular, with numerous companies creating home-made ices such as the Swansea area's Joe's Ice Cream or north Wales' Cadwaladr's.

Two traditional **cakes** are almost universal. Welsh cakes are flat, crumbling pancakes of sugared dough (a little like a flattened scone), while bara brith, a popular accompaniment to afternoon tea, literally translates as "speckled (with dried fruit) bread".

Menus featuring Welsh dishes can be found in numerous restaurants, hotels and pubs, many of which are part of **Wales the True Taste** (Cymru y Gwir Flas; w[walesthetruetaste.com](walesthetruetaste.com)), a government scheme to encourage local cuisine. Such establishments generally display a sticker in their windows.

Where to eat

If you're staying in a hotel, guesthouse or B&B, a hearty cooked breakfast (generally served 8–9am) will usually be offered as part of the deal, and may see you through the day. Evening meals are served from 6 to 10pm, though in rural areas, especially early in the week, you may find it difficult to get served after 8.30pm.

Cafés and **tearooms** (the terms are used pretty much interchangeably) can be found absolutely everywhere, and are generally the cheapest places to eat, providing hearty, cholesterol-laden breakfasts, a solid range of snacks and full meals for lunch (and occasionally, evening meals). Wales' steady influx of New Agers has seen the cheap and usually vegetarian **wholefood café** become a standard feature of many mid- and west Welsh towns.

Throughout the land, cafés and restaurants are also increasingly equipped with espresso machines, though barista competence levels are low.

Food in pubs varies as much as the establishments themselves. Competition has seen mediocre places sharpen up their act, and many pubs now offer more imaginative dishes than microwaved lasagne and chips. Most serve food at lunchtime and in the evening (usually until 8.30 or 9pm), and in many towns, the local pub is the most economical place (and, in smaller towns, sometimes the only place) to grab a filling evening meal. Relatively few Welsh hostelries have done the full gastropub conversion, but the standards in some pubs can now be very high.

Such places, along with bistros and restaurants, sport menus which rely extensively on fresh local produce. They can often tell you which farm the beef came from, and in coastal areas the chef may even know the fisherman.

The Cardiff brewery Brains has recently been buying up pubs around the country and smartening them up (cheap food, good beer and comfortable surroundings), but often robbing them of much individuality in the process.

People of all nationalities call Wales home and few towns of any size are without Indian or Chinese restaurants, though the likes of Japanese, French, Thai, American, Mexican and Belgian are limited to the more cosmopolitan centres.

Our restaurant listings include a mix of high-quality and good-value establishments, but if you're intent on a culinary pilgrimage, you'd do well to arm yourself with a copy of the annual Good Food Guide (Which? Publications), which includes detailed recommendations. Throughout this guide, we've supplied the phone number for all restaurants where you may need to book a table. In pubs and cafés you can expect to pay £6-10 for a main course, closer to £15 in good restaurants and around £20 in the very best places.

2. Drinking

As elsewhere in Britain, daytime cafés are not usually licensed to sell alcohol, and though restaurants invariably are, pubs remain the centre of social activity. The legal drinking age is 18, though an adult can order alcohol for someone aged 16 or 17 who is dining. Some places offer special family rooms for people with children, and beer gardens where younger kids can run free.

Pubs

Welsh pubs vary as much as the landscape, from opulent Edwardian palaces of smoked glass, gleaming brass and polished mahogany in the larger towns and cities, to thick-set stone barns in wild, remote countryside.

Where the church has faltered as a community focal point, the pub often still holds sway, with those in smaller towns and villages, in particular, functioning as community centres as much as places in which to drink alcohol. Live music – and, this being Wales, singing – frequently round off an evening. As a rule of thumb, if a pub has both a bar and a lounge, the bar will be more basic and frequently very male-dominated, while the lounge will tend to be plusher, more mixed and probably a better bet for a passing visitor.

Opening times vary but typically are Monday to Saturday 11am to 11pm, Sunday noon to 10.30pm (with many quieter places closed between 3 and 6pm, particularly throughout the week), with "last orders" called by the bar staff about fifteen minutes before closing time. Liberalization of licensing laws has allowed pubs to stay open later, but with the exception of city centres most places stick close to the standard hours.

What to drink

Beer, sold by the pint (generally £2.60–3.20) and half pint (half the price), is the staple drink in Wales, as it is throughout the British Isles. Traditionalists drink real ale, an uncarbonated beer, usually hand-pumped from the cellar but sometimes served straight from the cask; it comes in many varieties (some seasonal), including the almost ubiquitous deep-flavoured bitter, but sometimes mild, or dark as it is often known in Wales. Lager, which corresponds with European and American ideas of beer, is also stocked everywhere.

Also quite common Is the sweeter and darker porter. Irish stout (Guinness, Murphy's or Beamish) is widely available.

Among beers worth looking out for are the heady brews produced by Cardiff-based Brains, mainly found in the southeastern corner of Wales. Llanelli-based Felinfoel covers the whole southern half of Wales, with Double Dragon Premium bitter the aromatic ace in their pack. Crown Buckley, also based in Llanelli but owned by Brains, produces three excellent bitters and a distinctive mild.

Newer brews, such as Otley from Pontypridd, Evan Evans from Llandeilo and Purple Moose from Porthmadog, have won numerous awards.

Many pubs are owned by large, UK-wide breweries who sell only their own products, so if you are interested in seeking out distinctive brews, choose your pub carefully. The best resource for any serious hophead is the annual Good Beer Guide produced by CAMRA (the Campaign for Real Ale; wcamra.org.uk): if you see a recent CAMRA sticker in a pub window, chances are the beer will be well worth sampling.

As in other Celtic regions, cider has a huge following; look out for Orchard Gold (a traditional farmhouse apple cider) and Perry Vale (pear cider), both made by the Welsh Cider and Perry Company (Gwynt y Ddraig).

Pubs and off-licences (liquor stores) increasingly stock a growing range of Welsh spirits, such as Merlyn (cream liquor, similar to Baileys), Taffoc (toffee spirit), Five (vodka) and Penderyn (single malt whisky). There are also a number of Welsh wines, though you rarely see these offered on restaurant wine lists. Wines sold in pubs have improved considerably in recent years, although the best world selections tend to be found in the places serving good food.

Few restaurants have a good selection of wines by the glass, generally offering little more than a house white and a house red.

WALES

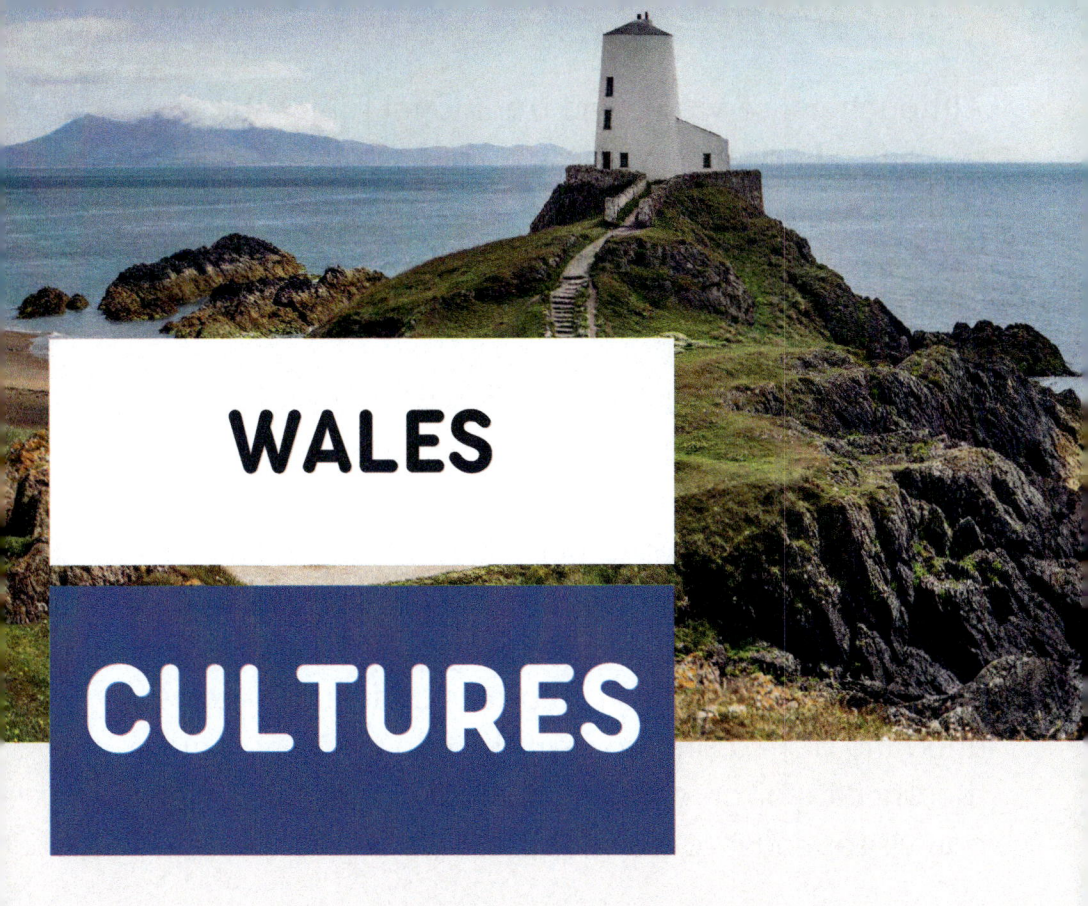

CULTURES

Although it is the wealth of places to visit - prehistoric sites, crumbling castles and wild landscapes - that brings tourists to visit Wales in the first place, they often leave championing the contemporary element. The cities and university towns throughout the country are buzzing with an understated youthful confidence and sense of cultural optimism, while a generation or two of "New Age" migrants has brought a curious cosmopolitanism to the small market towns of mid-Wales and the west.

Although conservative and traditional forces still sporadically clash with these more liberal and anarchic strands of thought, there's an unquestionable feeling that Wales is big enough, both physically and emotionally, to embrace such diverse influences.

Perhaps most importantly of all, Welsh culture is underpinned by an iconoclastic democracy that contrasts starkly with the establishment-obsessed class divisions of England. The Welsh character is famously endowed with a musicality, lyricism, introspection and sentimentality that produces far better bards and singers than it does lords and masters. And Welsh culture is undeniably inclusive: anything from a sing-song in the pub to the grandiose theatricality of an eisteddfod involves everyone – including any visitor eager to learn and join in.

1. Wales, the Land of song

"Praise the Lord! We are a musical nation," intones the Rev. Eli Jenkins in Dylan Thomas' masterpiece, Under Milk Wood. It's a reputation of which the Welsh feel deservedly proud. Although plucky miners singing their way to the pithead was the dewy-eyed fabrication of Hollywood (How Green Was My Valley), Wales does make a great deal more noise, and make it a great deal more tunefully, than most other small countries.

The country's male voice choirs, many struggling to survive in the aftermath of the decimation of the coal industry that spawned them, are the best-known exemplars of Welsh singing, but traditions go much further back, to the bards and minstrels of the Celtic age. Wales continues to nurture big voices and big talent: from the hip-swivelling Sir Tom Jones and show-stopping Dame Shirley Bassey to anarchistic rockers the Manic Street Preachers and young divas like Charlotte Church, Katherine Jenkins and Duffy.

2. Male voice choirs

Fiercely protective of its reputation as a land of song, Wales demonstrates its fine voice most affectingly in its ranks of male voice choirs. Although found all over the country, it is in the southern, industrial heartland that they are loudest and strongest. Their roots lie in the Nonconformist religious traditions of the seventeenth and eighteenth centuries, when Methodism in particular swept the country, and singing was a free and potent way of cherishing the often persecuted faith.

Classic hymns like Cwm Rhondda and the Welsh national anthem, Hen Wlad Fy Nhadau (Land of My Fathers), are synonymous with the choirs. Each Valleys town still has its own choir, most of whom welcome visitors to sit in on rehearsals. Ask at the local tourist office or library, and take the chance to hear one of the world's most distinctive choral traditions in full, roof-raising splendour.

The country's male voice choirs, many struggling to survive in the aftermath of the decimation of the coal industry that spawned them, are the best-known exemplars of Welsh singing, but traditions go much further back, to the bards and minstrels of the Celtic age. Wales continues to nurture big voices and big talent: from the hip-swivelling Sir Tom Jones and show-stopping Dame Shirley Bassey to anarchistic rockers the Manic Street Preachers and young divas like Charlotte Church, Katherine Jenkins and Duffy.

2. Male voice choirs

Fiercely protective of its reputation as a land of song, Wales demonstrates its fine voice most affectingly in its ranks of male voice choirs. Although found all over the country, it is in the southern, industrial heartland that they are loudest and strongest. Their roots lie in the Nonconformist religious traditions of the seventeenth and eighteenth centuries, when Methodism in particular swept the country, and singing was a free and potent way of cherishing the often persecuted faith.

Classic hymns like Cwm Rhondda and the Welsh national anthem, Hen Wlad Fy Nhadau (Land of My Fathers), are synonymous with the choirs. Each Valleys town still has its own choir, most of whom welcome visitors to sit in on rehearsals. Ask at the local tourist office or library, and take the chance to hear one of the world's most distinctive choral traditions in full, roof-raising splendour.

WALES

TRAVEL ADVICES

1. Costs

Wales is certainly not a cheap destination, but prices are generally lower than in many parts of England, particularly London. With the current weakness of the pound, many foreign visitors should find prices quite reasonable.

The minimum expenditure, if you're camping and preparing most of your own food, would be £20-25 per day, rising to £35-40 per day if you're using the hostelling network, some public transport and grabbing the odd takeaway or meal out. Couples staying at budget B&Bs, eating at unpretentious restaurants and visiting a fair number of tourist attractions are looking at £60 each per day – if you're renting a car, staying in comfortable B&Bs or hotels and eating well, you should reckon on at least £80 a day. Single travellers should budget on spending around sixty percent of what a couple would spend, mainly because single rooms cost more than half the price of a double. For more detail on the cost of accommodation, transport and eating, see the relevant sections.

VAT

Most goods in Britain, with the chief exceptions of books and groceries, are subject to a 20 percent Value Added Tax (VAT), which is almost always included in the quoted price. Visitors from non-EU countries can get a VAT refund when leaving the country on goods bought through the Retail Export Scheme: participating shops have a sign in their window.

Student and youth cards

The various official and quasi-official youth/student ID cards are of relatively minor use in Wales, saving only a few pence for entry to some sites. If you already have one, then bring it, but if you don't, it's barely worth making a special effort to get one.

Full-time students are eligible for the International Student Identity Card (ISIC, wisiccard.com), while anyone under 26 can apply for an International Youth Travel Card, which carries the same benefits. Both cost £9.

Several other travel organizations and accommodation groups also sell their own cards, good for various discounts. A university photo ID might open some doors, but is not as easily recognizable as the ISIC cards.

Tipping and service charges

In restaurants a service charge is sometimes included in the bill; if it isn't, leave a tip of 10–15 percent unless the service is unforgivably bad. Taxi drivers expect a tip in the region of ten percent. You do not generally tip bar staff – if you want to show your appreciation, offer to buy them a drink.

2. Tourist attractions

Many of Wales' most treasured sites – from castles, abbeys and great houses to tracts of protected landscape – come under the control of the privately run UK-wide National Trust or the state-run CADW, whose properties are denoted in the Guide by "NT" and "CADW".

Both organizations charge an entry fee for most places, and these can be quite high, especially for the more grandiose NT estates. We've quoted the standard adult entry price, but UK taxpayers are encouraged to pay the gift aid price, which adds around ten percent to the normal adult price, but through tax offsets gives the NT considerable benefit.

If you think you'll be visiting more than half a dozen NT places or a similar number of major CADW sites, it's worth buying an annual pass. Membership of the National Trust (t0844 800 1895, wnationaltrust.org.uk; £50.50, under-26s £23.50, family £88.50) allows free entry and parking at its properties throughout Britain. Sites operated by CADW (t01443 336000, wcadw.wales.gov.uk; £35, seniors £22, ages 16–20 £20, under-16s £16) are restricted to Wales, but membership also grants you half-price entry to sites owned by English Heritage and Historic Scotland.

CADW offers the Explorer Pass, which allows free entry into all CADW sites on three days in seven (adult £13.20, family £28), or seven days In fourteen (£19.85/£38.75). Entry to CADW sites is free for Welsh residents over 60: check their website to obtain a pass.

Many other old buildings, albeit rarely the most momentous, are owned by the local authorities, and admission is often cheaper. Municipal art galleries and museums are usually free, as are sites run by the National Museums and Galleries of Wales (wmuseumwales.ac.uk), including the National Museum and St Fagans National History Museum, both in Cardiff. Although a donation is usually requested, cathedrals tend to be free, except for perhaps the tower, crypt or other such highlight, for which a small charge is made. Increasingly, churches are kept locked except during services; when they are open, entry is free. (You'll normally be able to find a notice in the porch or on a board telling you where to get a key if the church is locked.) Wales also has a number of superb showcases of its industrial heritage, mostly concerned with mining and mineral extraction.

Keen birders might consider joining the RSPB, where membership (wrspb.org.uk; £36 a year) gives you free entry to its reserves throughout Britain.

Entry charges given in the Guide are the full adult rates, but the majority of the fee-charging attractions located in Wales have 10–25 percent reductions for senior citizens and full-time students, and 20–50 percent reductions for under-16s – under-5s are admitted free almost everywhere. Proof of eligibility is required in most cases. Family tickets are also common, usually priced just under the rate for two adults and a child and valid for up to three kids. Finally, foreign visitors planning on seeing more than a dozen stately homes, monuments, castles or gardens might find it worthwhile to buy a Great British Heritage Pass (£39 for 3 days, £69 for 7 days, £89 for 15 days, £119 for 30 days; w[britishheritagepass.com](britishheritagepass.com)), which gives free admission to over four hundred sites throughout the UK, over forty of them in Wales.

3. Climate

The climate is fairly consistent across Wales, though it is considerably wetter, and a little cooler along the mountainous spine, particularly in Snowdonia.

4. Electricity

In Britain, the current is 240V AC at 50Hz. North American appliances will need a transformer, though most laptops, phone and MP3 player chargers are designed to automatically detect and adapt to the electricity supply and don't need any modification. Almost all foreign appliances will require an adapter for the chunky British three-pin electrical sockets.

For details of how to plug your laptop in when abroad, phone country codes around the world, and information about electrical systems in different countries look at wkropla.com.

5. Emergencies and police

As in any other country, Wales' major towns have their dangerous spots, but these tend to be inner-city housing estates where you're unlikely to find yourself. The chief risk on the streets – though still minimal – is pickpocketing, so carry only as much money as you need, and keep all bags and pockets fastened. Should you have anything stolen or be involved in an incident that requires reporting, go to the local police station. The t999 (traditional British) or t112 (pan-European) numbers for police, fire and ambulance services should only be used in emergencies. There is also a non-emergency number for the police t101 (10p per call).

6. Entry requirements

Citizens of all European countries – other than Albania, Bosnia Herzegovina and most republics of the former Soviet Union – can enter Britain with just a passport, generally for up to three months. US, Canadian, Australian and New Zealand citizens can travel in Britain for up to six months with just a passport. All other nationalities require a visa, available from the British consular office in the country of application.

For stays longer than six months, check details on the UK Border Agency website (wind.homeoffice.gov.uk), where you can download the appropriate form. Do this before the expiry date given on the endorsement in your passport.

Embassy contact details are listed on the website of the Foreign and Commonwealth Office (wfco.gov.uk): look for links to "Find Embassies" and "Find a Foreign Embassy in the UK".

Tobacco: 200 cigarettes; or 100 cigarillos; or 50 cigars; or 250g of loose tobacco.
Alcohol: Four litres of still wine, plus one litre of drink over 22 percent alcohol, or two litres of alcoholic drink not over 22 percent, or another two litres of still wine.
You're also allowed other goods (including perfume) to the value of £390.

7. Gay and lesbian Wales

Homosexual acts between consenting males were legalized in Britain in 1967, but it wasn't until 2000 that the age of consent for gay men was made equal to that of straight men at sixteen. Lesbianism has never specifically been outlawed, apocryphally owing to the fact that Queen Victoria refused to believe it existed. In December 2005, civil partnerships between same-sex couples were legalized – marriage in all but name.

With such a rural culture, it's perhaps not surprising that Wales is less used to the lesbian and gay lifestyle than its more cosmopolitan English neighbour. That said, there's little real hostility, with the traditional Welsh "live and let live" attitude applying as much in this area as any other. Several Welsh musicians, academics, TV stars and politicians have come out in recent years, and no one's really batted an eyelid.

The organized gay scene in Wales is fairly muted. The main cities – Cardiff, Newport and Swansea – have a number of pubs and clubs, with Cardiff especially beginning to see a worthy and confident gay scene – a Mardi Gras festival in early September included – more in keeping with the capital's size and status. Details are given in the text of the Guide.

Out of the southern cities, however, gay life becomes distinctly discreet, although university towns such as Lampeter, Bangor and Wrexham manage support groups and the odd weekly night in a local bar, while Aberystwyth is a significantly homo-friendly milieu. The wgaywales.co.uk website is the best resource for gay and lesbian events, venues and accommodation, and has links to other relevant sites. Alternatively, there are some informal but well-established networks, especially among the sometimes reclusive alternative lifestylers found in mid- and west Wales. Border Women (who should surely have called themselves Offa's Dykes; wborderwomen.org) is a well-organized lesbian network for mid-Wales and the Marches.

8. Health

No vaccinations are required for entry into Britain. Citizens of all EU countries are entitled to free medical **treatment** at National Health Service hospitals; citizens of other countries are charged for all medical services except those administered by accident and emergency units at National Health Service hospitals. Thus a US citizen who has been hit by a car would not be charged if the injuries simply required stitching and setting in the emergency unit, but would be if admission to a hospital ward were necessary. Health insurance is therefore strongly advised for all non-EU nationals.

Pharmacies (known generally as chemists in Britain) can dispense only a limited range of drugs without a doctor's prescription. Most pharmacies are open during standard shop hours, though in large towns some may stay open as late as 10pm. Doctors' surgeries tend to be open from about 9am until early evening; outside surgery hours, you can turn up at the casualty department of the local hospital for problems that require immediate attention – unless it's a real **emergency**, in which case ring for an ambulance on t999 or t112.

9. Insurance

Wherever you're travelling from, it's a good idea to have some kind of travel insurance to cover you for loss of possessions and money, as well as the cost of any medical and dental treatment. Before paying for a new policy, however, it's worth checking whether you are already covered: some all-risks home insurance policies may cover your possessions when overseas, and many private medical schemes include cover when abroad. Students will often find that their student health coverage extends during the vacations and for one term beyond the date of last enrolment.

After exhausting the possibilities above, you might want to contact a specialist travel insurance company, or consider the travel insurance deal we offer. A typical travel insurance policy usually provides cover for the loss of baggage, tickets and – up to a certain limit – cash or cheques, as well as cancellation or curtailment of your journey. Most of them exclude so-called dangerous sports unless an extra premium is paid: in Wales this can mean whitewater rafting, windsurfing and coasteering, though probably not ordinary hiking. If you take medical coverage, ascertain whether benefits will be paid as treatment proceeds or only after return home, and whether there is a 24-hour medical emergency number. When securing baggage cover, make sure that the per-article limit – typically under £500 – will cover your most valuable possession. If you need to make a claim, you should keep receipts for medicines and medical treatment, and in the event you have anything stolen, you must obtain an official statement from the police.

10. Internet

Throughout Wales, almost all public libraries now have free internet access with several computers and wi-fi. Typically you just front up, and sign in for the next available half-hour or hour-long slot.

Cybercafés (where you can expect to pay £2–4 an hour) are a dying breed, supplanted by the plethora of free wi-fi hotspots at cafés and bars – the Wetherspoon pub chain, many Brains pubs and even McDonald's. Free wi-fi is also common (but not universal) at B&Bs and hotels.

11. Mail

Virtually all post offices (swyddfa'r post) are open Monday to Friday 9am to 5.30pm, Saturday 9am to 12.30pm. In small communities, you'll find sub-post offices operating out of a shop, but these work to the same hours even if the shop itself is open for longer. Stamps can be bought at post office counters and from a large number of newsagents and other shops, although often these sell only books of four or ten stamps. A first-class letter to anywhere in Britain (up to 100g) costs 46p and should arrive the next day; second-class letters cost 36p, taking two to four days to arrive. Postcards cost 68p to EU countries, and 76p to everywhere else.

12. Measurements

Like the rest of Britain, Wales is in very slow transition from imperial to metric measurements. Groceries are sold in packets quoted in grams and litres but usually in portions equivalent to a pound or a pint. Maps show mountain heights in metres but road distances are in miles and speeds in miles per hour. Petrol is sold by the litre. In pubs, beer is still sold in pints.

13. Money

The British pound sterling (£; punt in Welsh, and informally referred to as a "quid") is divided into 100 pence (p; in Welsh, c for ceiniogau). Coins come in denominations of 1p, 2p, 5p, 10p, 20p, 50p, £1 and £2. Notes come in denominations of £5, £10, £20 and £50. Shopkeepers will carefully scrutinize any £20 and £50 notes tendered, as forgeries are not uncommon.

Cards, cheques and ATMs

Most hotels, shops and restaurants in Wales accept the major credit, charge and debit cards, particularly Access/MasterCard and Visa/Barclaycard. American Express and Diners' Club are less widely accepted. Cards are even accepted at lots of B&Bs, though you should always be prepared to pay cash. Many businesses that do accept cards require a £10 minimum purchase. With a suitable PIN (ask at your bank before leaving home) your card will also enable you to get cash advances from most ATMs, though there may be a standard fee which makes it more cost-effective to withdraw larger sums. In addition, you may be able to make withdrawals from your home bank account using your ATM cash card – check before leaving home.

The safest way to carry your money is in travellers' cheques, available for a small commission (normally one percent) from any major bank. These can be exchanged at banks and bureaux de change and replaced if lost of stolen. Recognized brands – American Express, Thomas Cook, MasterCard and Visa – are accepted in all major currencies, but travellers' cheques (even in sterling) aren't accepted as cash.

Banks

Almost every Welsh town has a branch of at least one of the major banks: NatWest, Halifax, HSBC, Barclays and Lloyds TSB. As a general rule, opening hours are Monday to Friday 9 or 9.30am to 4.30 or 5pm, and branches in larger towns are often open on Saturday from 9am to 1pm. In the larger towns you may be able to find a bureau de change (often the post office), which will be open longer hours but may charge high commission.

14. Opening hours and public holidays

General shop hours are Monday to Saturday 9am to 5.30/6pm, although there's an increasing amount of Sunday and late-night shopping in the larger towns, with Thursday or Friday being the favoured evenings. The big supermarkets also tend to stay open until 8 or 9pm from Monday to Saturday, and open on Sunday from 10am to 4pm, as do many of the stores in the shopping complexes springing up on the outskirts of major towns.

Note that not all service stations are open 24 hours, although you can usually get fuel around the clock in the larger towns and cities. Also, most fee-charging sites are open on bank holidays, when Sunday hours usually apply.

In addition to the public holidays your travels around Wales may be disrupted by school holidays, when accommodation in popular areas (especially near beaches) is stretched by holidaying families. The main school holidays are two weeks around Christmas and New Year, two weeks around Easter, and six weeks from mid-July to early September. There is also a one-week break in the middle of each term, one usually falling in late May.

15. Phones

Given the near-ubiquity of mobile phones, most people don't have much need for public payphones (teleffon), which are operated by BT (wbt.co.uk), and are still found all over the place. Some also allow SMS text messaging (20p) and have internet access (£1 for 15min). Calls to anywhere in the UK (except to mobiles and premium numbers) cost 60p for the first 30 minutes then 10p for every 15 minutes thereafter. Most payphones in out-of-the-way places no longer take coins, forcing you to use credit and debit cards (UK calls 20p/min, plus a £1 connection charge), or account-based phonecards available from post offices and some shops. When buying such cards, read the small print, as there are often all manner of extra charges and penalties.

Call costs vary greatly depending on whether you are calling from a private land line, public pay-phone or the mobile network you are on. We've given call cost guidelines below.

To call Wales from outside the UK, dial the international access code (t011 from the US and Canada, t0011 from Australia and t00 from New Zealand), followed in all cases by 44, then the area code minus its initial zero, and finally the number.

16. Shopping

The quintessential Welsh memento is a lovespoon – an intricately carved wooden spoon that in centuries gone by was offered by suitors when courting. The meanings of the various designs range from a Celtic cross (symbolizing faith/marriage) to vines (growing love) and a double spoon (commitment), with dozens of others available. Prices range from a few pounds for a small version, to several hundred pounds for a large, elaborate spoon by a well-known carver. You'll find them in craft shops all over the country, including some dedicated solely to these ornaments.
Other unique items include some superb paintings, jewellery, leatherwork and screen-printing from arts and crafts galleries throughout Wales; some are run by the artists themselves, and you can watch them at work. Given that Wales has an estimated three to four times as many sheep as humans, it's not surprising that there are some wonderful woollen products available.

17. Smoking

Since 2007 smoking has been banned in restaurants, bars and clubs and on public transport. You'll now see clusters of die-hard smokers outside pubs and occupying café pavement tables in all weathers. Cigarettes are seldom on display (you'll have to ask for them) and may soon come in plain packaging.

18. Tourist information

Wales promotes itself enthusiastically, broadly through Visit Britain and more specifically through Visit Wales, both with extensive websites offering a wealth of free literature, some of it just rose-tinted advertising copy, but much of it extremely useful – especially the maps, city guides and event calendars.

Visit Wales and tourist offices

Visit Wales (aka Croeso Cymru: t0870 830 0306, wvisitwales.com) operates a central information service that's excellent for pre-trip planning, with a detailed website and plenty of free brochures which can either be downloaded or sent by mail. There is also representation at Visit Britain, 1 Regent St, London SW1Y 4XT (t020 8846 9000, wvisitbritain.com).

Tourist offices (usually called Tourist Information Centres or TICs) exist in many Welsh towns – you'll find their contact details and opening hours throughout the Guide. The average opening hours are much the same as standard shop hours, though in summer they'll often be open on a Sunday and for a couple of hours after the shops have closed on weekdays; opening hours are generally shorter in winter, and in more remote areas the office may well be closed altogether. All centres offer information on accommodation (which they can often book), local public transport, attractions and restaurants, as well as town and regional maps.

Areas designated as national parks (the Brecon Beacons, Pembrokeshire Coast and Snowdonia) also have a fair sprinkling of National Park Information Centres, which are generally more expert in giving guidance on local walks and outdoor pursuits.

Printed in Great Britain
by Amazon